# I Wish I Lived - WHEN GIDEON DID

### by
### Geoffrey T. Bull
### Illustrated by Chris Higham

ￜￜￜ *Pickering & Inglis*
LONDON — GLASGOW

Printed in Great Britain
ISBN 0 7208 2246-7
Cat. No. 11/3503

I sometimes wish a wish you know
Then all at once away I go
Across the snow-capped mountain tops
With leaps and bounds and such big hops,
My steps like giants, so swift and wide,
I take the rivers in my stride!
It's all so easy in the mind
You don't get half as tired, I find.

On such a journey once I came
To where the troubles were the same
As daddy talks about, at table,
When a people are not able
To control things as they ought;
When they never give a thought
To the God who cares for men,
No one can be happy then.

It was Palestine you know,
Many, many years ago;
When the people had no King
To decide on anything.
When they thought they'd like to do
Just the thing they wanted to.
'We are free,' they liked to say;
But too quickly came the day
When they all had to confess
They were in an awful mess.

People didn't pull together;
They became like leaf or feather
Blown about and tossed around
In the air and on the ground.
And when enemies came in
Not a battle could they win.
Now like slaves they worked for others,
Brothers, sisters, fathers, mothers,
Toiling, toiling in the sun,
Thus their work was never done.
And the little food they got,
Foreign soldiers stole the lot!

Soldiers from the land of Midian,
Coming in the days of Gideon
Took their barley and their wheat
While their men were reaping it.
So behind a winepress there,
Gideon threshed his in despair.

Oh, how sad his heart became
When he thought of all the shame
Sin had brought upon his nation
Who despised God's great salvation
When He brought them out of bond
From the dread of Egypt's darkness
To a land of milk and honey,
Asking neither price nor money.
But they wouldn't let God reign;
Sin they wanted, sin again.

'The Lord is with thee, Gideon,
Hiding wheat from Midian!'
'Twas an angel spoke the word,
'Trust in God and take your sword.
Break your father's idol now,
Shall God's people to it bow?'

Gideon took ten friends by night;
Did the work with all their might,
Threw the ugly idol down,
None but God would Gideon own.

'He must die,' the people said,
'Such a man must lose his head.'
But his father would not have it.
'Let the idol try and do it!
If he can, then he's the one . . .
If he can't—why kill my son?'
So they shouted very long
'Come on idol! You are strong!'
But 'twas such a useless thing;
Once again the Lord was King.

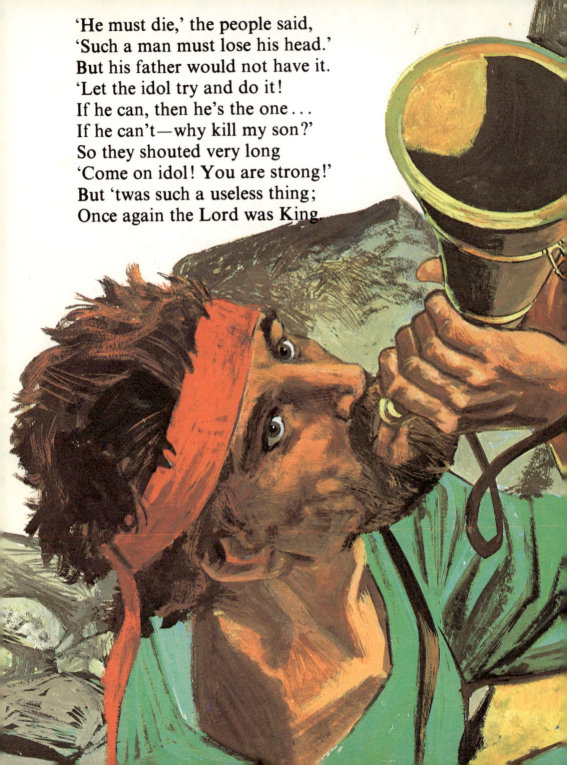

Gideon full of God's own Spirit,
Blew his trumpet, hurried to it.
Gathered up a host of men
Out of hill and dale and glen.

Then he prayed, 'Dear God, I ask
If I am to do the task,
If my people and their land
Shall be saved from Midian's hand,
Let, I pray, a sign be given
From Your Throne up there in heaven.

'First let dew be on this fleece,
Yet quite dry around it, please.'
In the morning it was so.
God was with him, he would go.
But once more he thought he'd try,
'Now Lord, let the fleece be dry
And the ground around it wet.'
So the Lord did so that night.

'Right!' said Gideon, 'Now I'm ready.'
But said God, 'You take it steady.
You have got too many men.
When the battle's won, why then,
You will say it was their might
Gained the victory, won the fight.'
'No, it *must* be by My hand.
Search out now a little band.

Let the thousands go back home;
Most of them don't want to come.
For the rest, see how they drink,
Some will bow down to the brink.
They're not soldiers—far too slack!
Foes would stab them in the back.
Let the men who drink and look
Eyes alert when at the brook
Lapping quickly from their hand,
Be My chosen little band.'

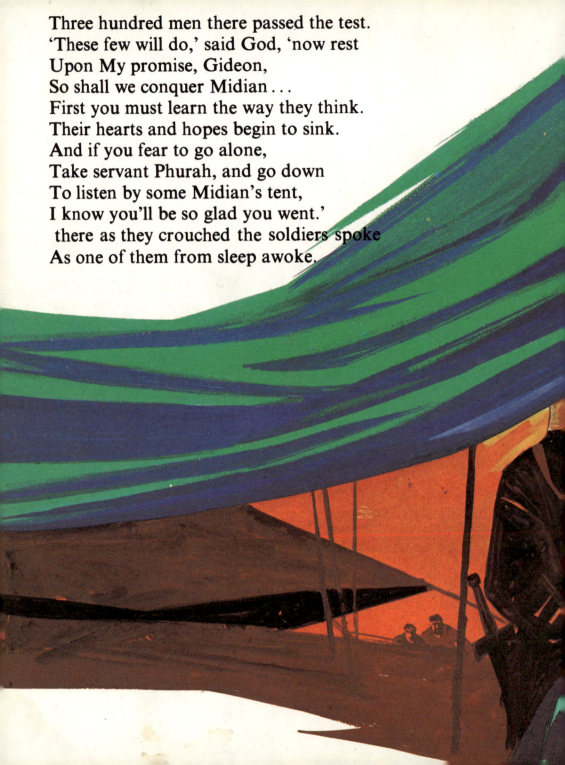

Three hundred men there passed the test.
'These few will do,' said God, 'now rest
Upon My promise, Gideon,
So shall we conquer Midian...
First you must learn the way they think.
Their hearts and hopes begin to sink.
And if you fear to go alone,
Take servant Phurah, and go down
To listen by some Midian's tent,
I know you'll be so glad you went.'
there as they crouched the soldiers spoke
As one of them from sleep awoke.

He told them of a dream he dreamed.
'You know', he said, 'to me it seemed
As if a little barley-cake,
The kind of thing poor people bake,
Came tumbling down upon my tent
And tore it open, made a rent,
Until it crumpled on the floor.
　　　Such was my dream,
　　　　　it was no more.'

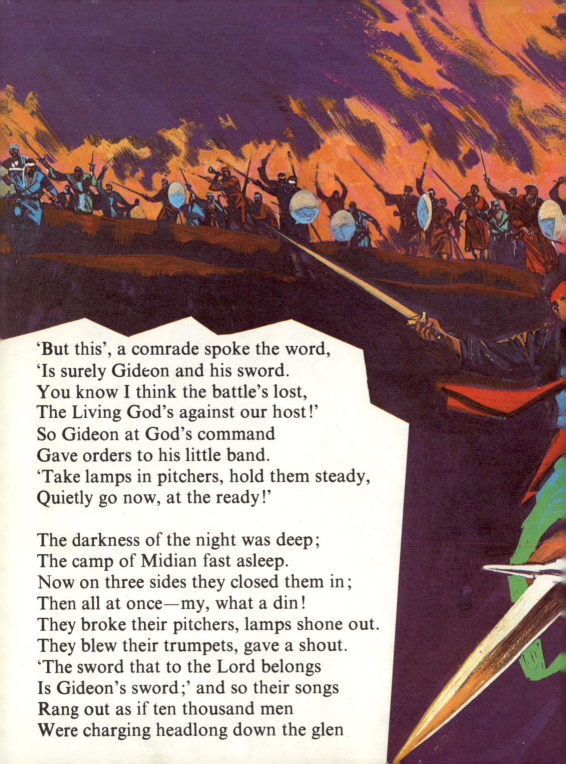

'But this', a comrade spoke the word,
'Is surely Gideon and his sword.
You know I think the battle's lost,
The Living God's against our host!'
So Gideon at God's command
Gave orders to his little band.
'Take lamps in pitchers, hold them steady,
Quietly go now, at the ready!'

The darkness of the night was deep;
The camp of Midian fast asleep.
Now on three sides they closed them in;
Then all at once—my, what a din!
They broke their pitchers, lamps shone out.
They blew their trumpets, gave a shout.
'The sword that to the Lord belongs
Is Gideon's sword;' and so their songs
Rang out as if ten thousand men
Were charging headlong down the glen

The Midianites got up and ran,
They started fighting man with man.
They did not have the slightest clue
Of who was friend or foe or who;
They simply fled into the night
Before the God of Israel's might.
It was a marvellous happening
When Gideon proved
the Lord was King.